The CABINETMAKERS

*A New England chair of the early 1700's,
fashioned in the Queen Anne style.*

COLONIAL CRAFTSMEN

The
CABINETMAKERS

WRITTEN & ILLUSTRATED BY

Leonard Everett Fisher

BENCHMARK BOOKS

MARSHALL CAVENDISH
NEW YORK

Benchmark Books
Marshall Cavendish Corporation
99 White Plains Road
Tarrytown, New York 10591-9001

Library of Congress Cataloging-in-Publication Data
Fisher, Leonard Everett.
The cabinetmakers / written and illustrated by Leonard Everett Fisher.
p.   cm. — (Colonial craftsmen)
Reprint. Originally published: New York : Franklin Watts, 1966
Includes index.
Summary: A history of woodworking craftsmen in colonial America,
describing their tools, materials, and workmanship.
ISBN 0-7614-0479-1 (library binding.)
1. Cabinetwork—United States—History—Juvenile literature. 2. Cabinetmakers—
United States—Juvenile literature. 3. Furniture, Colonial—United States—Juvenile
literature.[1. Cabinetwork. 2. Cabinetmakers. 3. Furniture—United States.
4. United States—History—Colonial period, ca. 1600–1775.] I. Title.
II. Series: Fisher, Leonard Everett. Colonial craftsmen.
TT197.F55   1997   338.4'7684104'097309032—dc20   96-16606   CIP   AC

Printed and bound in the United States of America

3   5   6   4   2

Other titles in this series

A Short History

"**A**LL THE COUNTREY IS OVER-growne with trees," wrote Captain John Smith when he saw the Virginia coast of North America in 1607.

George Percy, a gentleman-adventurer, was also impressed by the same Virginia forests. He wrote, "Wheresoever we landed upon this River, wee saw the goodliest Woods, as Beech, Oke, Cedar Cypresse, Wal-nuts, Sassafras. . ."

John Smith, George Percy, and 102 other men founded the first permanent English settlement in America amid the woods they wrote about. Their tiny colony was called Jamestown in honor of James I, King of England, who was then ruling.

In the American wilderness there seemed to be no end to the trees. This great forest was valuable, as lumber could be sent back to England and used to make everything from ships and cannon mounts to cradles. Moreover, the lives of the settlers themselves depended on the trees. Logs were needed not only for fuel, but to repair the ships, to build houses and a fort, and to use

The *HISTORY*

"All the countrey is overgrowne with trees...."

in making and replacing lost or broken barrels, chests, wheels, tools, tables, chairs, gunstocks, knives and spoons, and other equipment.

The only woodworking craftsmen among the band of Englishmen to land on American soil in 1607 were several carpenters and at least three coopers, or barrel makers and menders. Like many of the others, the carpenters came to find treasure, become rich, and return to England as quickly as possible.

The coopers came for a different reason. No doubt they sought riches, but there was something more than that. Without these men the three ships that made the voyage to Jamestown could not have left England. In those days every English ship that set out on a long trip was required by law to have one master cooper in her crew. His job was to watch over the casks that held the ship's provisions and drinking water. He spent most of his time seeing to it that not one drop of precious liquid leaked from the containers.

Working with the carpenters and coopers, the Jamestown adventurers used the wood of the

Virginia forests to make and repair many of the things they needed. What little furniture they had in the early years they knocked together themselves.

Soon other woodworking craftsmen arrived in Jamestown, but during the early years of the settlement, just staying alive was the main business of everyone. No one was interested nor had he time to spend in making any furniture except what was badly needed — a table, perhaps, or a few rough stools, or a plain chest or cupboard where belongings could be stored.

Thirteen years after the beginning of Jamestown another group of Englishmen, the Pilgrims, founded Plymouth Colony on Massachusetts Bay. They brought very little furniture with them in their ship, the *Mayflower.* It was already crammed with the crew and the settlers themselves, and with the tools, clothing, food, water, rope, weapons, gunpowder, and other supplies they needed. Because most of the Pilgrims were craftsmen of one kind or another they were better prepared to make their home in the New World than were the Jamestown settlers. But at first

The *HISTORY*

they too found that keeping alive was their main job. They lived in rough shelters and dugouts and had little use for furniture. Gradually, however, they became used to their new way of life, and from the trees in the forest around them they built a church, a strong fort, and sturdy houses. Then they made the furniture they needed. It was of a simple kind, and practical for the hard uses of their everyday life. Cupboards, chests, large, heavy tables, benches, stools, beds, and a very few chairs made up most of it.

A great deal of the Pilgrims' furniture may have been made by John Alden, together with Kenelm Winslow, another furniture maker who lived near Plymouth for a time. Or perhaps each of them worked alone. John Alden had come to Plymouth as the *Mayflower*'s twenty-one-year-old master cooper. A member of the ship's crew, he had been hired by the Pilgrims, according to law, to watch over the barrels of provisions and drinking water. Although at first he was not one of their number, John Alden decided to remain with the Pilgrims in Plymouth, where he married Priscilla Mullens. There he learned to make fur-

In early colonial days no one
had either the tools or the skill
to make any but simple furniture.

niture. But in the early colonial days no one had either the tools or the skill to make any but simple furniture. It was strong, heavy, and above all, practical.

The HISTORY

Because many of the colonists had come from England their furniture followed English styles. Fashions that were the rage in London soon found their way to America. In the late seventeenth century many skilled workmen moved from Europe to England. Among them were furniture makers. These European furniture makers built pieces that were lighter than the English furniture. The European pieces were decorated with curves, with veneers of wood, and with intricately put together patterns of ivory and of woods and shells of various kinds. Many of the chests and tables had carefully fitted drawers in a great variety of sizes.

This European work was much finer than the English work up to that time, and was done with great skill and artistry. Many of the English craftsmen learned the improved new methods. From about 1685 on, some English furniture makers began to call themselves *cabinetmakers*

and organized themselves into an association, or guild. Earlier in the century, furniture had been made by men called *joiners,* who also did work joining pieces of wood together to make doors, window frames, paneled walls, and floors. For a long time to come, though, many furniture makers still called themselves joiners, and advertised themselves as such on the signs above their shops.

By about 1700 many cabinetmakers began to come from England to work in America. They brought knowledge of the new English furniture styles with them. The hardship of the early days of settlement was easing in the colonies. Now people had more time to enjoy themselves and they were becoming more prosperous. They read more and they wrote more, so they needed desks, or combinations of desks and bookcases called secretaries, and they needed small tables that would hold a light. They entertained their friends more, and they needed tea tables. People had more possessions and they liked to keep some of their treasures in cabinets.

The cabinetmakers, with their improved meth-

Clamp

The *HISTORY*

ods of workmanship, met all these demands and they began to produce lighter furniture that was decorative as well as useful. They followed English styles, but each craftsman added little touches of his own. The furniture had an American quality, even though today it is called William and Mary period furniture or Queen Anne period furniture after the English monarchs of the time.

Between 1750 and 1783, when the colonial American cabinetmakers were in greatest demand, the most popular style of furniture made in America was similar to or an exact copy of the English Chippendale style. Thomas Chippendale, a London cabinetmaker, had become the most celebrated maker of fine furniture in England. His book of designs, *Gentleman and Cabinet-Maker's Director,* published in 1754, was used by almost every colonial cabinetmaker of the time.

Although colonial cabinetmakers borrowed English fashions, changing them slightly here and there, they used the native American woods: walnut, chestnut, beech, pear, gum, apple, sycamore, cherry, cedar, pine, and tulip. Perhaps the

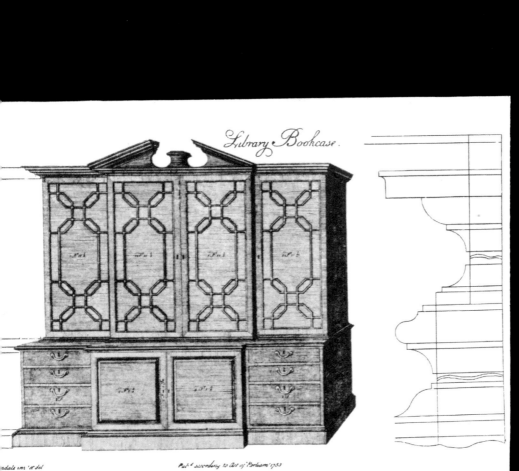

Library Bookcase.

only exception was mahogany, a hard but workable wood found in the West Indies, Mexico, and South America. Chippendale used mahogany with such marvelous results that some colonial cabinetmakers imported and used it, too.

The **HISTORY**

The American cabinetmakers became so skillful that some of them labeled their work much as an artist would sign his paintings. Colonial American cabinetmakers, like the cabinetmakers of the Old World, were generally well-educated, well-trained craftsmen. Their trade demanded not only a perfect knowledge of various woods, but a sense of proportion and form and a good understanding of geometry and other kinds of mathematics. Since most cabinetmakers designed at least some of their own pieces, they not only had to know a great deal about the styles of design and ornament, from that of the ancient Greeks to that of Thomas Chippendale, but they also had to know certain principles of engineering in order to make their furniture stand in perfect balance and remain strong. Besides all this, they were artistic men who were as interested in creating a thing of lasting beauty as they were in making useful furniture.

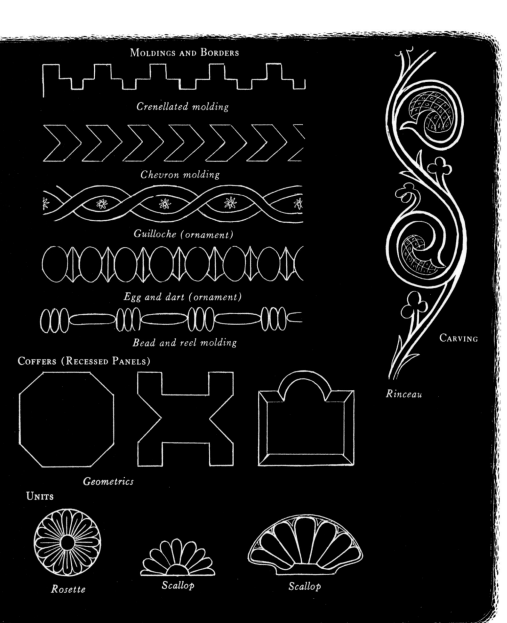

MOLDINGS AND BORDERS

Crenellated molding

Chevron molding

Guilloche (ornament)

Egg and dart (ornament)

Bead and reel molding

COFFERS (RECESSED PANELS)

Geometrics

UNITS

Rosette

Scallop

Scallop

CARVING

Rinceau

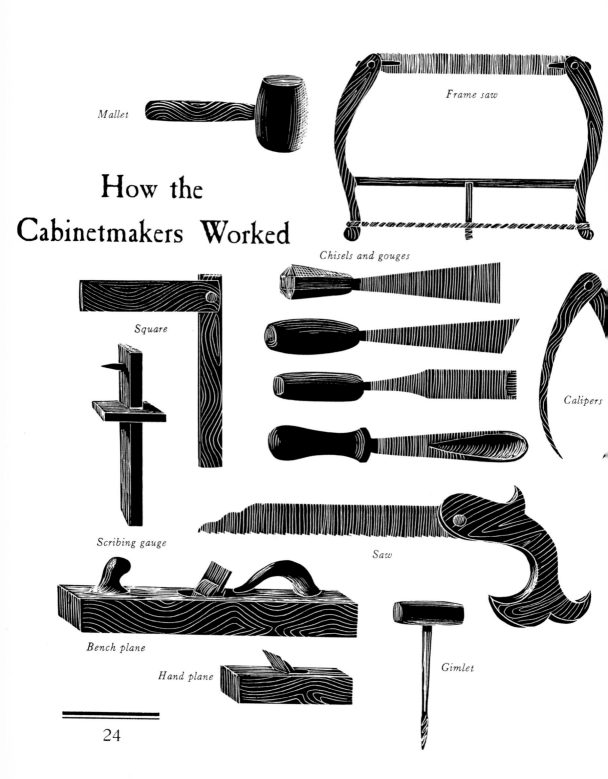

How the
Cabinetmakers Worked

Mallet

Frame saw

Chisels and gouges

Square

Calipers

Scribing gauge

Saw

Bench plane

Hand plane

Gimlet

ALL THE COLONIAL AMERICAN FUR-niture makers, both the early joiners and the later cabinet-makers, used special skills in their work. A good maker of fur-niture, whether he was a joiner or a cabinetmaker, knew how to choose the right woods for the particular job he had to do, and he could use his many tools to shape the wood so that the various parts of the piece would fit to-gether perfectly and lastingly. But a joiner did not have the variety of tools nor was he expert enough to make the really fine furniture a cabi-netmaker created.

The cabinetmaker's first task was to see that all his tools were in excellent working order and that he had every tool he would possibly need. Each of the many tools in his shop had its own special function, and the cabinetmaker had to know just how, where, and when to employ each one.

For the most part, the hand tools of the colo-nial American cabinetmakers were much like those that are used today. There was a great as-

Great wheel lathe *Cabinetmaker's shop*

Bow drill

*A cabinetmaker shapes a
furniture part on a
three-speed treadle lathe.*

sortment of different-shaped saws, chisels, planes, gimlets, augers, hammers, files, clamps, braces, and bits. Most of these tools were made in England.

The simple machine tools used by the colonial cabinetmaker were also not unlike the high-speed electrically powered tools used by the modern cabinetmaker. There were *lathes,* or machines for shaping, or *turning,* a piece of wood by holding it firmly in place and rotating it against a cutting tool. The slender, curved leg of a cabinet or chair was made on a lathe. There were several types of lathes in the colonial cabinetmaking shop. They were all worked by hand or foot. The *great wheel lathe* was kept in motion by a young apprentice who rotated a large drive wheel with a hand crank. The *treadle lathe* was worked by the craftsman himself, who had to keep pressing a pedal to keep the machine in motion. If the cabinetmaking shop was a large one in which several different kinds of woodworking craftsmen were employed, the craftsman who worked at the lathe was usually a *turner.* If the shop was small, the cabinetmaker himself worked the lathe, or else

Pulleys

1 2 3

Drive cord

Drive wheel

Treadle

LEF

he sent the part out to be made at a *turning shop*.

Another important piece of equipment was the workbench. And again, the workbench was not unlike those of today. It was a large, thick, heavy wooden table to which were attached *vises,* or clamps, to hold the wooden parts steady while they were being fashioned.

The wood used by the colonial American cabinetmaker was as important as were his tools. Though there was an abundance of native wood in the forests, not all this was suitable for the making of furniture. Certain woods called *primary woods* were best for the outside or showy part of the furniture piece. Some other woods, called *secondary woods,* were more suitable for the basic construction of the piece. They made up parts of the furniture that were seldom seen, such as the backs of cabinets, the sides of drawers, and the frames of couches.

During most of the colonial period the primary wood most popular with the American cabinetmakers was black walnut, although a good deal of oak was used in the very early days. Walnut was easy to saw, shape, and carve. It was hard

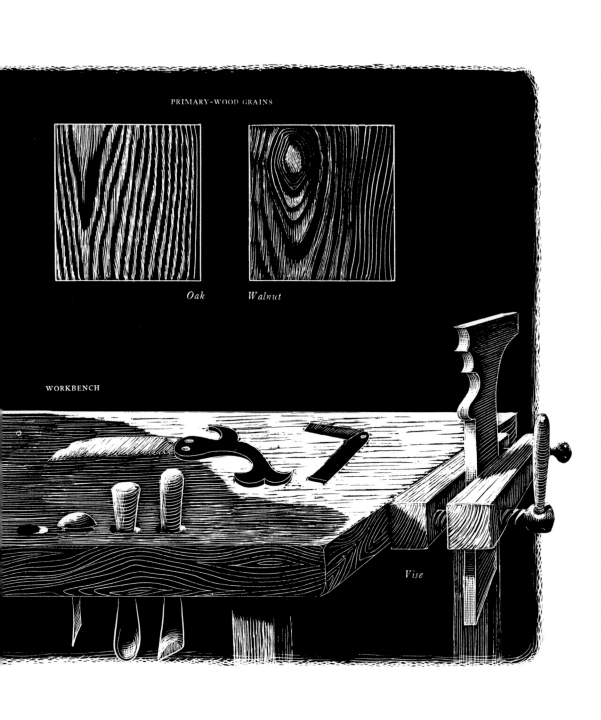

PRIMARY-WOOD GRAINS

Oak   *Walnut*

WORKBENCH

Vise

*The vise grips a furniture
part while the
cabinetmaker shapes it.*

enough not to scratch easily and strong enough not to warp. When it was stained, waxed, and polished it was beautiful to look at. Two other primary woods favored by the colonial cabinetmakers were maple and wild cherry.

The *TECHNIQUE*

Secondary woods, such as pine, white cedar, and tulip, usually were cut from those trees that grew near the cabinetmaker's shop. The secondary woods were less expensive than the primary woods.

Once the cabinetmaker had chosen the proper woods for a piece of furniture, he shaped all the parts separately, according to the patterns he himself had worked out or according to those already drawn in a book of designs. Next followed the two steps that in the end decided whether or not the piece would be strong and pleasing to look at: putting the parts firmly together and finishing the wood.

The points where the separate parts were fitted together were called *joints*. If they were not perfectly made, the furniture would be so crooked that not only would it wobble but it would soon fall apart.

Sometimes a *lap joint* was made by cutting the ends of two pieces to half thickness and laying one piece over the other. At other times a *butt joint* was made by fitting the squared end of one piece against the squared end of another. A more complicated joint was the *mortise and tenon*. One part was cut with a square tongue, or *tenon*, at the end of it. In the other part, to be attached, a square hole, or *mortise*, was cut. It fitted the tenon, or tongue, perfectly. The two parts were joined by slipping the tenon into the mortise. This joint was used for fitting secondary woods at right angles.

Similar to the mortise and tenon joint was the *dovetail joint*. Cut into the end of one part was a tenon shaped like a dove's spread tail — wider at the outer end. A slot to match this tenon was cut out of the part to be attached. The tenon was then fitted into the slot, to form the joint, ordinarily used in the making of drawers.

The *rabbet, tongue and groove,* and *miter* were other types of joints used by the colonial cabinet-makers. Never did a skilled master cabinetmaker use metal nails to fasten joints together. In fact,

The **TECHNIQUE**

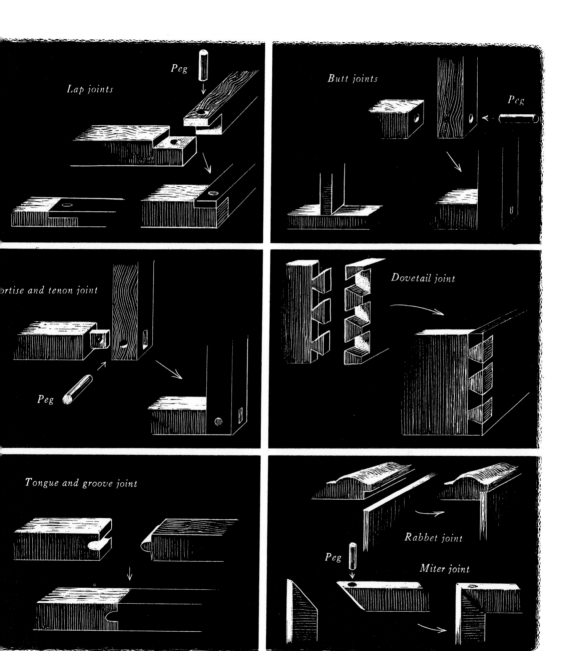

Lap joints

Peg

Butt joints

Peg

Mortise and tenon joint

Peg

Dovetail joint

Tongue and groove joint

Rabbet joint

Peg

Miter joint

The *TECHNIQUE*

he almost never used nails at all. He depended on the exact fit of a precisely made joint. If anything else seemed necessary to add strength to the fitted parts, he might use warm glue made from the boiled skin and bones of animals. Or sometimes he drove wooden pegs into a joint to make it stronger.

When the piece of furniture had been put together, the cabinetmaker turned his attention to *finishing,* or staining, shellacking, waxing, and polishing the primary woods. A finish protected the wood against scratching and dampness, cold and heat; it kept the wood firm and in good condition for a lifetime of use; it brought out the interesting, often beautiful, natural patterns in the grain. When he first chose the wood to be made into furniture the cabinetmaker had these things in mind. As he was careful in fitting a joint, so too was he careful in matching the grains of two separate pieces of wood. If the wood were not carefully matched, an unpleasant patchwork of patterns would result, with the grains going every which way.

The early joiners usually carved their pieces,

The *TECHNIQUE*

or painted parts of them red or black to make them more attractive. While the later cabinetmakers often used some carving too, they depended more on the beauty of the wood and their skill in forming and fitting the parts into a final shape that was pleasing.

There were many different methods of finishing a wood piece. More often than not, these methods produced a finish that was shiny and smooth as glass. They all made use of stains or dyes, varnishes and shellacs, turpentine, oil, and beeswax.

The kind of finish decided on usually depended on the cabinetmaker's likes and dislikes and on the type of wood he used. Whatever the finish, the craftsman first had to prepare the surface of the wood. He did this by smoothing it painstakingly with either sandpaper or glass paper.

In colonial days the most popular method of finishing furniture was first to stain or tint it with a dye in order to deepen its natural color and bring out the pattern in the grain of the wood. Sometimes powdered chalk was added to the stain in order to fill tiny pinholes that possibly

had appeared in the wood. When the stain was dry, the surface of the wood was sanded again. Next the cabinetmaker gave the stained wood a coating of varnish made by dissolving copal resin in turpentine, or he gave it a coating of shellac made by dissolving lac in alcohol. In either case the coating was allowed to dry and the surface was again sanded. The cabinetmaker continued this process until the wood had a very hard, mirror-like surface. He then melted beeswax in a pot of turpentine (about one part of wax to four parts of turpentine). While this mixture was still hot, he brushed a very thin coating of it onto the varnished or shellacked and sanded wood. The wax not only added more protection to the wood, but it also cut down the bright glare from the varnish or shellac. The waxed wood was then polished or buffed to a low sheen.

Sometimes the cabinetmaker *oiled* the wood instead of varnishing and shellacking it. He did this by pouring a mixture of boiled linseed oil and turpentine onto the wood, then wiping the mixture off and allowing the surface to dry. When it was dry, the cabinetmaker sanded the wood or

The *TECHNIQUE*

rubbed it for hours with his bare hands. He continued to pour and rub until the wood had just the shine and smoothness he wanted.

When all the finishing was complete, the cabinetmaker added whatever wood, iron, or brass knobs, drawer pulls, locks, hinges, or handles were necessary. All this hardware was attached with expensive handmade brass screws. If the furniture was to be upholstered, or fitted with padding and cloth of some kind, the cabinetmaker himself did the job with a hammer and brass tacks, or else a craftsman called an *upholsterer* did the work for him.

The colonial American cabinetmakers produced their handmade furniture for whoever would buy it, or they made it on special order. The cabinetmakers of the large, well-populated cities were busy enough to spend all their time making furniture of one kind or another. But those cabinetmakers who lived and worked in the less populated outlying districts were not as lucky. To add to their incomes many of them turned to making wooden coffins. Some of them found the coffin-making business so profitable that in time they

gave up cabinetmaking and became undertakers, or funeral directors.

Be that as it may, the skill of the cabinet-makers of eighteenth-century colonial America was truly amazing. Many of the pieces they fashioned, some fancy, some plain, are still in use today, two hundred years later. The sturdiness of this furniture, to say nothing of its fine proportions, skilled craftsmanship, and simple beauty, seems to reflect the solid strength of the colonial Americans who laid the foundations of the free republic that was to follow.

Chair table, New England, 1675, said to have been owned by Peregrine White, who was born on the Mayflower. Its back tilts down to form a table-top (see photograph at right). Furniture like this was useful to the early settlers since it helped save space. (Metropolitan Museum of Art)

Cupboard (around 1650), possibly from Plymouth. Built-in closets were rare in the homes of the early settlers, and cupboards like this were useful to housewives. (Metropolitan Museum of Art)

This blockfront secretary (around 1770) shows all the cabinetmaker's skill at beautiful decoration and at fitting drawers and shelves. (Metropolitan Museum of Art)

Side chair, Chippendale style, around 1765. (Metropolitan Museum of Art)

A child's desk, Queen Anne style, about 1725. (Metropolitan Museum of Art)

Blockfront chest of drawers, made by John Townsend of Newport, R. I., in 1765. (Metropolitan Museum of Art)

Carved oak chest, New England, around 1675. (Metropolitan Museum of Art)

Index

LEONARD EVERETT FISHER is a well-known author-artist whose books include *Alphabet Art, The Great Wall of China, The Tower of London, Marie Curie, Jason and the Golden Fleece, The Olympians, The ABC Exhibit, Sailboat Lost,* and many others.

Often honored for his contribution to children's literature, Mr. Fisher was the recipient of the 1989 Nonfiction Award presented by the *Washington Post* and the Children's Book Guild of Washington for the body of an author's work. In 1991, he received both the Catholic Library Association's Regina Medal and the University of Minnesota's Kerlan Award for the entire body of his work. Leonard Everett Fisher lives in Westport, Connecticut.

DATE DUE
